I Asked...
He Gave

Cora Lee Smart-Crisco

PublishAmerica
Baltimore

First printing

ISBN: 1-4137-9120-4
PUBLISHED BY PUBLISHAMERICA, LLLP
www.publishamerica.com
Baltimore

Printed in the United States of America

Dedication

To my beloved family:
my husband,
my children and their spouses,
my grandchildren and their spouses,
my great-grandchildren,
my step-children and their spouses,
and my step-grandchildren.

Acknowledgements

I am so very thankful to my Lord and Savior, Jesus Christ, for inspiring every word of this book. I am also thankful to Him for answering my prayers, especially for giving me the *words to say* to witness for Him. He is such a loving God, and I love Him so very much.

Gregory Alexander Smart, my grandson, thank you for designing the front cover of my book and also for helping to proofread. I love you, Alex.

I could not have gotten everything ready for submission of my manuscript had it not been for my sweet daughter, Jackie Jernigan, who helped me put everything together, Brian Helms, who helped me with my computer, and Cindy Sasser, who prepared announcement labels. Thanks! You all are the best!

Lastly, I would like to thank my step-son, Terry, who found my publisher. I love you, Terry.

Rebirth

One night as I was asleep on my bed,
I had a dream, a vision in the night.
As I looked upward toward the sky,
There I saw a beautiful butterfly.

With wings so brilliantly colored bright,
It was a most beautiful, wonderful sight.
God's rebirth of a sinner's soul
Was displayed to me as my dream did unfold.

The meaning of a butterfly is rebirth.
And rebirth you are granted on this earth.
If only you will confess your sins
And call on Jesus and turn to Him.

He is the only way to gain
Your soul's salvation and lose all pain.
Give your heart to Him today.
And in Heaven you'll live, forever to stay.

September 1, 1993
5:00 a.m.

The Presence of God

So often as I trod along,
I lift my voice to God in song.
I love to praise and worship Him
Even when my road seems dark and dim.

Sometimes I'm on a mountain top
So happy and so free.
And then I'm in the valley
Feeling as alone as I can be.

At times like these
When I feel so alone,
I kneel and pray
And ask God to make His presence known.

I know He will never fail me,
And all I need to do is seek
His holy presence on my knees
When I feel so alone and weak.

April 18, 1994

Face to Face

Someday when I stand before Jesus,
When I see Him face to face,
I will thank Him for His mercy,
And I will thank Him for His grace.

Most of all I will thank Him
For hanging on that old tree.
I can never ever thank Him enough
For what He did at Calvary.

Oh! How humble and unworthy I feel
When I think of Calvary.
How my Savior bled and died that day
When He gave His life for me.

He could have called His angels.
He could have been set free.
But He chose to go to the cross to show
His miraculous love for me.

I cannot wait for the day to come
When I see Him face to face.
It should have been me who died for my sins,
But my Jesus took my place.

June 2, 1994
10:45 p.m.

Our Day

NKJV, 1 Peter 4:5 — They will give an account to Him who is ready to judge the living and the dead.

Do you know that we will all have our day in court?
When we stand before Jesus and give our report?
It will be an account of our lives here on earth
Everything that has happened since the time of our birth.

We will have to confess everything that was bad,
Everything that we did to make Jesus sad.
There are so many times when I know I had a part
Of sinning against Him and breaking His heart.

I wish I could erase the sins that I've done
Against my Lord Jesus, the Holy One.
But I know that He has forgiven me
When He took my sins on Calvary.

If you are not having a daily walk with Him,
And you think you can commit a little sin,
Please realize that there is no *little* sin,
That all sin is of the same importance to Him.

Please hear and be sure that our day will come
When we will stand before God as He sits on His throne.
I am longing for that precious day to come
When forever I will live in my heavenly home.

June 8, 1994
10:00 p.m.

I Shall Be Satisfied

NKJV, Psalm 17:15—As for me, I will see Your face in righteousness; I shall be satisfied when I awake in Your likeness.

Father, I want to be more like You
As I go along my way.
I want to wake up every morning
And seek Your perfect will for my day.

I want to perceive others
Better than I ever have.
I want to look for the good in them
And not look for the bad.

I want to speak to everyone
As I meet them on the street.
I want the Light of Jesus
To shine through me when we meet.

I want to keep a smile on my face
Instead of a great big frown.
I want to tell others about Jesus
As I travel all around.

I want to love everybody
With Your agape love.
I want You to be pleased
As You look down on me from above.

Dear Heavenly Father, I just want
To have a daily walk with You.
I want to feel Your holy presence
As I so often do.

And, Dear Father, when it's my time
To see Your face in righteousness,
I shall be satisfied
When I awake in Your likeness.

June 14, 1994
4:00 p.m.

God Is No Respecter of Persons

God is no respecter of persons.
It doesn't matter where you start.
He doesn't look at the outside.
He looks straight into your heart.

He looks into the innermost part.
He doesn't look at your skin.
It doesn't matter what color you are.
He died to save all from sin.

God is no respecter of persons.
He made us all from the same mold.
He didn't make some of us from metal,
And the others were not made from gold.

Sometimes we get *all puffed up*,
And think we are better than another.
That's when we need to take a long look at *me*.
We are no better than our brother.

God said if we didn't have love for all
No matter what they had done,
Then we would not inherit the Kingdom of Heaven
And live with Him in our heavenly home.

He did not say we had to love their ways,
But we do have to love their soul.
I know that sometimes they don't do what you like
And that sometimes they are very bold.

But Jesus went to the cross before there was *us*
To forgive us from our sins.
So don't you think you could find it in your heart
To forgive them and be more like Him?

So when you see someone on the street
And you think they are not quite like you,
Remember, God is no respecter of persons.
Be sure to do what you know God would do.

June 14, 1994
12:00 p.m.

Disciples

NKJV, John 20:20-21—When He had said this, He showed them His hands and His side. Then the disciples were glad when they saw the Lord. So Jesus said to them again, "Peace to you! As the Father has sent Me, I also send you."

When Jesus called His disciples
From their work to go with Him.
He said, "If you will follow Me,
I will make you fishers of men."

They each laid down their work
Each time He called out to them.
They left everything behind.
In faith, they followed Him.

He called them to be His witnesses,
To tell others how to gain life with Him.
That if first they would seek the Kingdom of God,
Everything else would be added to them.

Jesus has called us to be disciples, too,
To go out and witness for Him.
We are to tell others that, to have eternal life,
We must be cleansed from sin.

We must believe that Jesus
Is the beloved Son of God.
We must believe that He died
And was raised, as it says in His Holy Word.

We must ask Him to come into our heart,
And save us from our sin.
We must give Him complete control of our life,
To earn a heavenly home with Him.

Are you witnessing for Jesus every day
As our Father has told us to do?
He has called us just as He called the twelve
To be His disciples, too.

June 26, 1994
3:15 p.m.

Too Busy for God

Are you caught up in the *fast lane*, so to speak,
That your time with Jesus has become so weak?
You let the cares of this world take His place,
Because you are going at such a fast pace.

Have you no time for Jesus?
Have you carelessly shut Him out?
Do you never think about Him,
As you go here and about?

Don't you know it grieves my Savior
To see you live the way you do?
Won't it be sad when before Him you stand,
And He says, "Depart from me. I never knew you."

When that day comes, it will be too late;
You will not have another chance, so please don't wait.
I would not want my Lord to say to me,
"Why were you too busy to have time for Me?"

We seem to have time to do everything we want to do.
We always find time as one day goes into two.
Days fly by, and still we won't give Jesus any time;
We have too many other things on our mind.

Dear Friend, it is time you cleared your mind
Of all other things and give my Lord some time.
If you don't, then it will be too late.
Jesus will already have sealed your fate.

I'm not trying to scare you,
But, then, maybe I should
If that is what it takes
To make my words understood.

If you don't make time for Jesus
Before the end times come,
Then you will not get a chance
To share in my heavenly home.

My dear friend, please make time
For my sweet Jesus to share your day
So that, when He comes to gather His flock,
He will take you home, too, with Him to stay.

July 10, 1994
11:30 p.m.

The Potter

NKJV, Isaiah 64:8 — But now, O Lord, You are our Father; We are the clay, and You our potter; And all we are the work of Your hand.

Jesus is the Potter,
And we are the clay.
He molds us and makes us
In His image every day.

I know He is not through
With his job of molding me
Because I do not measure up
To what He wants me to be.

I do not spend enough time
Seeking God's will for me.
I do not stay on my knees enough
Praying to my Father, you see.

Why are we so negligent
When it comes to God's Holy Son?
How can we expect God's blessings
When we do not seek the Holy One?

If we want to get to know Him
As I know I want to do,
We will have to spend more time praying
And seeking Him the whole day through.

Remember, He is our Potter,
And we are the work of His hand.
So let Him mold us in His image
According to His holy, divine plan.

July 12, 1994
6:15 p.m.

Unity

NKJV, Psalm 133:1—Behold, how good and how pleasant it is for brethren to dwell together in unity!

Our Heavenly Father wants us
To live together in unity.
He does not want unforgiveness
To ever be between you and me.

It makes His heart so very sad
To see how His children fuss and fight.
Why can't we live together in harmony
And make everything that's wrong right?

We could, if we would only let
Our Father control our life,
Turn everything over to Him.
Then there would be no more troubles or strife.

When we try to control our life,
To settle all the discord,
Everything gets all out of shape
When we don't put our trust in the Lord.

The Lord is so pleased with us
When we forgive one another
And never hold any anger
Against one of our brothers.

We are all brothers and sisters
In the family of the Lord.
He tells us to keep the peace
All throughout His Word.

If Jesus could forgive us
For crucifying Him to save our sins,
Why is it so hard for us
To forgive others and call them friends?

The next time you get upset
And say things to others that are wrong,
Just turn your eyes to Jesus,
And soon all the anger will be gone.

Let's all live together
In perfect unity.
We will all be one in Christ,
One big, happy family.

July 14, 1994
3:00 a.m.

Sing Praises

NKJV, Psalm 147:1 — Praise the Lord! For it is good to sing praises to our God; For it is pleasant, and praise is beautiful.

Praise the Lord!
Sing praises to His holy name!
For the Lord is so good.
His love will always be the same.

Sing to our God!
Sing His praises. Lift your voice to the sky;
He inhabits our praises.
He hears from on high.

The Lord loves the praises
From His children who truly love Him.
Show Him your love.
Be faithful, do not sin.

Sing unto the Lord.
Let our God hear your voice.
The angels in Heaven praise Him.
Oh! How they rejoice.

They make a beautiful sound
As their voices are raised in song.
Let Jesus hear your voice.
Make it loud and strong.

Oh! how beautiful
Is the sound of our praise.
When it reaches the sky
As our voices in song we raise.

Let everyone praise the Lord.
Praise Him Who sits on the throne.
Sing praises, loud and clear,
To our God, the Omnipotent One.

July 19, 1994
3:15 a.m.

God's Gifts

God, help us to live one day at a time and enjoy each gift that you have given us. Help us to be glad and rejoice in each new day.

The gifts of God
Are so sweet and free.
There is no cost
To you or to me.

Jesus paid the price
That dark day on Calvary
When we hung Him to die
On that cruel, rugged tree.

Dear Father, my Lord
In Heaven above,
I just want to thank You
For Your unending love.

Father, help us to receive
The many gifts that You give,
The gifts that are free,
Given to help us live.

The best gift of all
Is salvation, full and free,
That You gave to us
When You died on that tree

And then when You were raised
On the third day
To join our Heavenly Father
For our reunion day.

What a day that will be
When I see You face to face
To fall on my knees
To thank You for Your mercy and grace.

Dear Jesus, I can never repay
The debt that I owe,
But I know You already paid it
A long, long time ago.

July 23, 1994
8:45 a.m.

City Not Built by Man

I can't wait to go to that city;
That city not built by man.
That beautiful, heavenly city
Built by God; by His almighty hand.

Can't you just envision its beauty?
Too beautiful for our eyes to behold
With God's own perfect beauty.
Oh! To walk on those streets of pure gold.

When Jesus went back to Heaven,
He promised us that He
Was going to prepare a mansion,
A perfect place for you and for me.

How I long to see my heavenly home
That Jesus has built for me.
It doesn't have to be a mansion.
I just want to be close to Thee.

I want to see my loved ones,
The ones who have already gone home.
But most of all I want to see Jesus
And worship around His throne.

If you want to go to that city,
That city that was not built by man,
Then call upon Him, confess your sins,
And come along, go home with me to that land.

July 23, 1994
2:00 p.m.

A New Name

NKJV, Revelation 2:17 — He who has an ear, let him hear what the Spirit says to the churches. To him who overcomes I will give some of the hidden manna to eat. And I will give him a white stone, and on the stone a new name written, which no one knows except him who receives it.

NKJV, Revelation 3:12 — He who overcomes, I will make him a pillar in the temple of My God, and he shall go out no more. I will write on him the name of My God and the name of the city of My God, the New Jerusalem, which comes down out of heaven from My God. And I will write on him My new name.

Our God has promised
To the ones who overcome
A white stone He will give us
When we come before His Throne.

On this white stone
There will be written a new name,
A name known only to us.
What a joy to proclaim!

Won't it be wonderful
To stand before Him?
If we have given Him our heart
And His Holy Spirit lives within.

He tells us He will also write on us
The name of the city, New Jerusalem.
We will never go out again
But dwell forever with Him.

I can hardly wait
When my new name He gives.
And I go to that city
With Him forever to live.

July 24, 1994
1:45 a.m.

Come to Me

NKJV, Matthew 11:28-30 — Come to Me, all you who labor and are heavy laden, and I will give you rest. Take My yoke upon you and learn from Me, for I am gentle and lowly in heart, and you will find rest for your souls. For My yoke is easy and My burden is light.

When you are lonely
And burdened down with care,
Just look up to Jesus
For He is always there.

You don't have to go
Through this world alone.
Just call upon my Savior.
He will hear from His throne.

He is so gentle,
So loving and kind.
He is so tender.
He will give you peace of mind.

You just can't imagine
How much He loves you.
He will take all your burdens
And will carry you through.

Learn from my Savior
How to find rest in Him.
Each day will go easier
When you learn to lean on Him.

He will hear your prayers
And will answer each one.
Won't you seek Him today?
Please don't try it alone.

Just walk with my Father,
One day at a time.
You will find sweet rest for your soul
In a world that is so unkind.

My God is the only one
Upon whom you can depend.
Come to Him today and learn.
He will carry you to the end.

July 25, 1994
4:15 a.m.

Be Still and Know That I Am God

*NKJV, Psalm 46:10—Be still, and know that I am God; I will be
exalted among the nations, I will be exalted in the earth!*

*NKJV, Isaiah 2:11—The lofty looks of man shall be humbled, the
haughtiness of men shall be bowed down, and the Lord alone shall
be exalted in that day.*

In this world so busy with life
As each day we hurriedly trod,
God in Heaven looks down on us
And says, "Be still. Know that I am God."

Are you too busy to pause and seek Him?
Do you stop each day to lift a prayer?
Or do you go busily on your way,
Not even realizing that He is waiting there?

Are you too concerned with *you*,
Too busy to take just a minute or two
To stop and exalt our Lord on High,
Who has given *everything* to you?

Don't get too *important* and hung up on you,
For God will bring you down if you do.
He says the proud will all be bowed down,
With their faces bowed low to the ground.

Even the trees will sing His praise.
And even the rocks will cry out.
All the world will come to the place.
Ever*ything* and *everyone* His praises will shout.

So stop! Be still! Know that He is God.
Take time to praise Him as you go your way
Because the day is coming when we all see Him.
And He, alone, will be exalted in that day.

July 27, 1994
5:15 a.m.

Paul

NKJV, Acts 26:29 — And Paul said, "I would to God that not only you, but also all who hear me today, might become both almost and altogether such as I am, except for these chains."

Paul used to persecute Christians
Each and every day
Until the Lord blinded him
Along the Damascus way.

The Lord got Paul's attention
When He brought him to his knees.
The Lord will get our attention, too,
If to Him we do not please.

The Lord told Ananias
To go and lay hands on Paul.
As soon as he did, the scales fell away,
And he could see one and all.

God had a great work for Paul,
Just as He does for you and me.
We are to witness to others
And tell them how they, too, can be set free.

Free from the bonds of Satan,
Who is lurking around everywhere.
All we have to do is confess our sins
And ask Jesus to come in our hearts in prayer.

Paul followed closely behind Jesus
And did His every command.
He told everyone he saw about Jesus
And tried to make them understand.

He told them how much Jesus loved them
And how they should love Him, too.
He told them that there is but *one God*
And to worship Him in spirit and truth.

Oh! How I would like to be more like Paul,
To walk closer to God every day.
Please, Dear Jesus, draw me close to You,
And never, never let me stray.

I want to meet Paul up in glory,
When we all gather around God's throne.
I want to thank him for telling us in God's Word
What we must do to find our way home.

July 28, 1995
1:50 p.m.

I Can't Wait

I can't wait until the day
When my Jesus comes to take me home.
No more troubles will I have,
Nowhere else will I have to roam.

I can't wait until I get to walk
On those streets of purest gold.
To see all my family and friends
And hear all the stories that will be told

About what it's like to live there
In that Heavenly place so sweet,
To have His loving hand upon them
When they kneel at His precious feet.

I can't wait until I see sweet Jesus,
And I look upon His dear face,
To have Him put His arms around me,
The One who saved me by His amazing grace.

I will look for you when I get there
As I am walking from place to place.
Please don't disappoint me, please be there,
Because I want to see your angel face.

I can't wait until we walk hand in hand
With our Lord beside the Crystal Sea,
Never more to be separated.
Please be there to walk with me.

July 30, 1994
12:50 p.m.

Don't Wait Too Long

Do people not realize
That there is a God above
Who is looking down at them
With a heart filled with love?

It saddens His heart to see
How they are living today.
They never think about Him.
They want to live *their* way.

All they want to do is to have a *good* time.
They think *good times* are what is real.
Do they ever take time to stop to think
That this is not our Father's will?

Do they ever think about God
As they are running from town to town,
Drinking and *living* it up
While He is looking down?

The day will come when they
Will need His tender touch.
Oh! That they would only realize
He loves them so very much.

He won't let them go on much longer
Because time is running out.
The end is very near.
And that's reality without a doubt.

What will He have to do
To make them change their act?
Please, Dear Father, show them mercy,
And open their eyes to the fact

That judgment is at the door.
So, please, Dear Lord, make them see
That, unless they turn to You,
Hell will be their destiny.

July 31, 1994
2:15 a.m.

The Lord of Everything

NKJV, Psalm 104:24—O Lord, how manifold are Your works! In wisdom You have made them all. The earth is full of Your possessions—

The marvelous works of God!
Oh, praise His holy name,
For He is the Creator of all.
Let all the world proclaim.

How wonderful are Your works, Oh, Lord,
In Heaven and on earth below.
Let men give thanks for Your goodness,
For all the blessings that daily flow.

I lift my heart in praise
To my wonderful Savior above.
I thank Him for all things
Given through His majestic love.

Let all men declare His works
With joyful songs of praise.
Let all men worship the King
While holy hands to Him are raised.

I will exalt and praise Your name,
O wondrous King of kings.
For You are my Lord and Savior;
The Lord of *everything*.

August 4, 1994
6:10 a.m.

The Armor of Light

The night is far spent;
The day is at hand
When the Lord will appear
With His angel band.

You will hear the trumpet sound
Very loud and clear.
You will know in an instant
That the time is here.

Will you be ready?
Will you be looking for Him?
Or will you still be living
In the mire of your sins?

The Lord tells us in His Word
To put on the armor of light.
We should all *stand ready*,
Be it day or night.

When the sound of the trumpet
Will awaken even the dead,
Will you be standing ready
With nothing to dread?

Will you be looking up
Toward the eastern sky,
Ready to go with Him
To the sweet bye and bye?

Please be ready and waiting;
Put on your armor of light.
It will be a shouting time
When we dress in robes of white.

It won't be long now.
He's standing by the throne,
Waiting for the Father to say,
"Son, go bring my children home."

August 8, 1994
4:00 a.m.

The God Who Forgives

NKJV, Isaiah 55:7—Let the wicked forsake his way, And the unrighteous man his thoughts; Let him return to the Lord, And He will have mercy on him; And to our God, For He will abundantly pardon.

NKJV, Psalm 99:8—You answered them, O Lord our God; You were to them God-Who-Forgives, Though You took vengeance on their deeds.

Our God in Heaven is so awesome.
He is such a forgiving God.
All we have to do is come to Him,
For He tells us so in His Word.

He tells the wicked to turn from sin,
To open their heart and invite Him in.
He will cleanse every wicked sin they have done
If they will confess them all to the forgiving One.

God will abundantly pardon
Through His mercy and His grace.
And then on Resurrection Day,
When they see Him face to face,

They will have nothing to fear
When He calls their name.
They can stand before Him
And will not have to be ashamed,

For their sins will already be forgiven
By the God-Who-Forgives.
All their sins are hidden under the blood,
And forever with Him they will live.

August 10, 1994
4:45 a.m.

The Star of Bethlehem

The Star of Bethlehem
Shone down from above
On the Babe who had come
To show us God's love.

It was all in God's plan
The night of the Child's birth.
He sent His Beloved Son
To save all the earth.

The tiny little Baby
Who lay in a manger bed
Was born to be a sacrifice
And His blood to shed.

What a marvelous part
Of God's plan He shared with us
When Mary, the chosen mother,
Gave birth to Jesus.

Dear Jesus in Heaven above,
I can never thank you enough
Because You came so willingly
To give Your life for us.

Why can't the *world* see
How the supreme sacrifice
Was given by Holy God
To save their life.

Dear Lord, please make them see
How for us you showed Your love
That night when the Star shone bright
On Bethlehem from above.

August 13, 1994
1:00 p.m.

The Words to Say

NKJV, Jeremiah 1:9 — Then the Lord put forth His hand and touched my mouth, and the Lord said to me: "Behold, I have put My words in your mouth."

So many times I bowed on my knees
And prayed to my Father above.
So many times I asked the Lord
To let me witness of His love.

I prayed that He would use me
To witness for Him every day.
I prayed that He would also
Give me the words to say.

Little did I know when I prayed this
How the words would come.
Little did I know how He would let me
Tell others about a Heavenly Home.

I never dreamed it would be
In the form of poems, you see.
Because I could never write poems.
The words would never come to me.

Sometimes now the words come hard.
Then I know it must be me.
I have learned at these times I have to
Patiently wait on Thee.

I did not dream He would use me
In such a powerful way
When I prayed to be His witness,
When I prayed for the words to say.

August 16, 1994
2:00 a.m.

It's Just Jesus and Me

When I pray to Jesus my Lord,
I know He hears my voice
Because He answers my prayers.
Oh! How my soul does rejoice.

How unworthy I feel
When before Him I kneel
To lift praises to Him
And beg forgiveness for sins.

It's just Jesus and me
When I kneel and call to Him.
He is the Holy One
Who died to cover my sins.

He died on Calvary.
He shed His blood to cover me.
I praise His Holy name
Because He set my spirit free.

He is worthy to be praised.
He is my Lord and King.
He's the Master of my soul.
He is my Everything.

I love to come in prayer
And kneel down before His throne.
I magnify His name.
I am one of His own.

It's just Jesus and me.
He's my Savior, I know.
The more I lift His name,
The sweeter His blessings flow.

August 17, 1994
2:35 a.m.

If You Miss Heaven

If you miss Heaven,
It will be a sad thing.
You will never hear
The many angels sing.

But that is not
The most important thing.
You will never get to serve
Jesus, my Lord and King.

You will never get to
Worship at His feet.
You will never get to hear
His voice so sweet.

You will never get to
Receive your crown of life.
You will never see the end
Of turmoil or strife.

It will be such a sad day
When you stand before Him and hear,
"Depart from Me, I never knew you.
You have no home here."

Please! Don't miss Heaven.
Ask Jesus to come into your heart today.
He will cleanse you and save you,
And forever with Him you will stay.

August 21, 1994
3:05 p.m.

Don't Be Surprised

NKJV, Jeremiah 5:4—Therefore I said, "Surely these are poor, They are foolish; For they do not know the way of the Lord, The judgment of their God."

NKJV, Jeremiah 8:7—Even the stork in the Heavens knows her appointed times; And the turtledove, the swift, and the swallow observe the time of their coming, But My people do not know the judgment of the Lord.

Don't be surprised at what you see
Happening here and there.
Don't be surprised when you hear of
Earthquakes, floods, and fires everywhere.

The Lord tells us that He will judge
The world in His time.
He also says His people
Will not recognize the signs.

Why is He sending a judgment?
Because this world is deep in sin.
Men have become so evil
They have turned their backs on Him.

How long do you suppose our God
Will let this evil world stand
When the wickedness of men
Is seen all over the land?

His church is His people,
And, if they are walking with Him,
They will have nothing to fear.
Our God will take care of them.

God says in His Word that His judgment
Will begin at the house of the Lord.
Do you believe Him?
Do you believe His Word?

If you do and you read it daily,
You will know that judgment has already begun.
So don't be surprised at what happens
From now until our God is done.

August 22, 1994
2:25 p.m.

He Is Risen

NKJV, 1 Peter 1:20-21—He indeed was foreordained before the foundation of the world, but was manifest in these last times for you who through Him believe in God, who raised Him from the dead and gave Him glory, so that your faith and hope are in God.

Thank God that He is risen.
He did not stay in the grave.
He arose in just three days
To show the world how to be saved.

He was there in Heaven with the Father
When God revealed His plan
That Jesus would come as a Baby
Then would die to save the soul of man.

Satan thought that he had won
That day at Calvary.
He didn't know that Jesus
Would live again for you and me.

Jesus arose from that old grave
To show us that we could live again.
The Bible says it is appointed once for all to die,
But we can live again just like Him.

Thank You, Dear Father, for your plan,
That Jesus' blood covers all sin.
Thank You that He is risen
And one day we will live again.

August 24, 1994
12:45 p.m.

Treasures in Heaven

NKJV, Matthew 6:19-21—Do not lay up for yourselves treasures on earth, where moth and rust destroy and where thieves break in and steal; but lay up for yourselves treasures in Heaven, where neither moth nor rust destroys and where thieves do not break in and steal. For where your treasure is, there your heart will be also.

Treasures are all in Heaven.
They are not here on this earth.
Things that are treasures to some
Turn out to be of no worth.

Our Father in Heaven tells us
Not to lay up treasures here
But to lay them up in Heaven,
For they are worth much more there.

He isn't talking about money,
For you will not need money there.
He's talking about the condition of your heart
And of the way you show Him you care.

He says where you lay up your treasure,
There your heart will also be.
There is no doubt about it;
Life on this earth is not for eternity.

Don't try to gather treasures here
While you are neglecting God.

Money will be worth nothing
When on Heaven's streets you trod.

So don't lay up treasures on this earth,
For they won't last very long.
But lay up your treasures in Heaven.
They will be *priceless* around God's throne.

August 25, 1994
3:20 a.m.

He Is Faithful

NKJV, I Thessalonians 5:24 — He who calls you is faithful, who also will do it.

NKJV, Philippians 1:6 — being confident of this very thing, that He who has begun a good work in you will complete it until the day of Jesus Christ;

The One Who called you is faithful,
So you also be true to Him.
He has called you for a special work
To complete until He comes back again.

No matter what your calling,
Do not let Him down.
He has begun a good work in you.
Be faithful! Add a star to your crown.

We know that all of our works
Do not earn our way home.
But the things we do here on this earth
Will be judged around God's throne.

He Who calls you is faithful.
He will give you the strength to endure
Anything that comes against you
While you are doing His work here.

You can be sure that the good work
He has called you to do will be done
If you are as faithful as He
Until Jesus comes back to take us home.

August 26, 1994
5:05 a.m.

One Day Very Soon

There is coming a day very soon
When Jesus returns for us.
We shall see Him in all of His glory
And all of His righteousness.

When the Eastern skies burst open
As Gabriel sounds the alarm,
The Mighty Son of God
Will come again from upon His throne.

Lift your eyes toward Heaven.
Be ready! Be looking for our King.
And all of His Holy angels
With Him He will bring.

The graves will begin to burst open,
And bodies will begin to fly
To meet our blessed Lord and Savior
Up there in the sky.

Then the ones who are His who are living
Down here on this earth below
Will quickly rise up to meet them
And away we will all go.

You! Be ready! Don't miss it
When Jesus comes back for His bride.
It will be one day very soon
When on wings we all glide.

Be about our Father's business.
Keep witnessing to others until then.
And, when that day comes, a day very soon,
We will be going home to live with Him.

August 28, 1994
12:25 a.m.

Jesus Made the Way

NKJV, Hebrews 9:12 — Not with the blood of goats and calves, but with His own blood He entered the Most Holy Place once for all, having obtained eternal redemption.

NKJV, Hebrews 10:10 — By that will we have been sanctified through the offering of the body of Jesus Christ once for all.

NKJV, Hebrews 10:12 — But this Man, after He had offered one sacrifice for sins forever, sat down at the right hand of God.

Jesus made the way for us
To live forever with Him
When He so willingly gave His blood
To cover all our sins.

We could never be made perfect
With burnt offerings from year to year.
Burnt offerings could never take away our sin.
That's why God sent His Son here.

Jesus had to die only once
As a sacrifice for us.
He went to the cross to give His all.
He is love, that man, Jesus.

It doesn't take the blood
Of goats and calves, you see.
It took the blood of my precious Jesus,
Which He gave at Calvary.

I wonder why the world can't see
What Jesus did for them.
He made the way, *the only way*
That we can live eternally with Him.

August 30, 1994
2:50 a.m.

Our God Will Provide

NKJV, Psalm 105: 39-43 — He spread a cloud for a covering, and fire to give light in the night. The people asked, and He brought quail, And satisfied them with the bread of Heaven. He opened the rock, and water gushed out; It ran in the dry places like a river. For He remembered His holy promise, And Abraham His servant. He brought out His people with joy, His chosen ones with gladness.

No matter what our need,
Our God will provide.
He never breaks a promise.
He's always by our side.

His chosen people of Israel
Murmured and complained,
But our God did not forsake them.
He took care of them just the same.

Our God went before them
In a pillar of cloud by day
And in a pillar of fire by night
To guide them on their way.

He gave them quail to eat
And bread from Heaven above.
Water came out of the rock.
He showered them with His love.

We have an awesome God!
He will keep us safe from harm
If we daily walk with Him
And lean on His precious arms.

He will save the world from sin
If in humbleness we will come
And seek His wonderful face
And turn to God's Holy Son.

Oh! Praise the name of Jesus,
Our Savior and our King.
He *will* provide for us
If we give Him our everything.

September 5, 1994
1:50 a.m.

More of You, Less of Me

Dear Father, I pray, as I bow on my knees,
Let there be more of You and less of me.
As I go along from day to day,
Let others see You, not me, along the way.

Please keep me as humble as I can be.
Never let *me* get in the way of Thee.
All I want is for the world to see
More of You and less of me.

Dear Jesus, I desire to do Your perfect will.
I know sometimes that is hard, but still
I want to be as much like You as I can be.
Let the world see more of You and less of me.

Lord, let me witness for You every day.
Please keep giving me the words to say.
Please hide me behind the Cross of Calvary.
Let them see more of You and less of me.

I love you, Dear Jesus. You are my King.
You are my Savior, my God, my everything.
I give You my life as I long to see
More of You and less of me.

September 13, 1994
11:35 p.m.

The Patience of Job

NKJV, Job 19:25-27 - For I know that my Redeemer lives, And He shall stand at last on the earth; And after my skin is destroyed, this I know, That in my flesh I shall see God, Whom I shall see for myself, And my eyes shall behold, and not another. How my heart yearns within me!

Oh! If we could have the patience of Job
To wait upon the Lord.
If only we would trust what He promises
In His Holy Word.

Job was faithful no matter what came.
He was faithful to the end,
Even when his friends came one by one
And tried to discourage him.

He would not listen to what they said.
Their words were empty to him.
They did not have the faith of Job
To know that God would always be there for them.

Job tried to tell them all
The outcome of the wicked man,
That they would know God's judgment
And feel the wrath of His almighty hand.

Satan thought that he had Job,
That Job would curse God and die.
But as God knows us all, He knew Job,
And that was the reason why

God let Satan come against him
With boils and sores and such.
Satan persecuted Job with all he had,
But that was not enough.

Job would not give in.
He did not let Satan get the best of him.
He trusted in Almighty God
And kept the faith until the end.

The Lord accepted Job
Because Job was faithful to Him.
He accepted the prayers of Job
When he prayed for his friends.

Job died at a ripe old age.
God restored everything to him and more.
If only we could be more patient like Job,
What blessings we could have in store.

September 18, 1994
4:25 a.m.

Precious Names of God

NKJV, Deuteronomy 32:3-4 — For I proclaim the name of the Lord:
Ascribe greatness to our God. He is the Rock, His work is perfect;
For all His ways are justice, A God of truth and without injustice;
Righteous and upright is He.

Majesty! That is Who You are.
You are the bright and morning star.
Holy! Holy is the one.
Omnipotent! All-powerful is the Son.

Mighty God! I praise Your holy name.
Eternal! You will always be the same.
Master! You are my Lord and King.
Jesus! Creator of all things.

You are the Lamb of God.
You are the Everlasting Word.
Savior! The keeper of my soul.
Wonderful! Magnificent to behold.

Alpha and Omega! The Beginning and the End.
Redeemer! The cleanser of all sins.
Lord! The Lord throughout eternity.
Love! The greatest love to me.

Rock! You are the solid rock
Wonderful Counselor! The comforter of the flock.
Teacher! The breaker of the bread.
Resurrection and Life! The raising of the dead.

There's no one who can come near
With my God I hold so dear.
You are my Lord, the Truth and the Way.
I will praise Your name each and every day.

September 19, 1994
12:55 a.m.

For You and I

NKJV, Isaiah 53:7—He was oppressed and He was afflicted, Yet He opened not His mouth; He was led as a lamb to the slaughter, And as a sheep before its shearers is silent, So He opened not His mouth.

NKJV, Luke 23:34—Then Jesus said, "Father, forgive them, for they do not know what they do." And they divided His garments and cast lots.

My blessed Lord and Savior
Died a cruel death at Calvary.
He opened not His mouth as He
Bore our sins so silently.

He hung there upon that tree
Without uttering a word
While they beat Him and mocked Him;
Only their cruelty was heard.

He hung between two thieves
Who truly deserved to die,
But my precious Jesus
Hung there for you and I.

He is my blest redeemer.
He is the holy Lamb.
Little did the soldiers know
They were crucifying the great I AM.

In three days, He was raised
To rejoin His Father above.
He promised when He went away
To return for His beloved.

It won't be long now before He returns
From His throne up on High.
Please be ready when that day comes,
For He's coming back for you and I.

September 21, 1994
1:35 a.m.

I Won't Give Up

I won't give up, no, I won't give up,
For the Lord has promised me
That, one day, one day not far away,
He will save my family.

They don't know nor can they guess
What my Lord has in store for them.
So many blessings will they receive,
When they fall on their knees and worship Him.

No more excuses for staying away
From the meeting place of God.
No more excuses for not picking up
And reading God's Holy Word.

The Holy Spirit will live in their hearts
And will guide them through each day.
They will come to know Him like I do
As He gently leads them along their way.

I won't give up until this day comes.
I will stay down on my knees.
I will keep praying for their salvation,
For I know my Lord hears me.

And when that day comes and He answers this prayer,
What a glorious day that will be!
That's why I won't give up; no, I won't give up
Because I want them to go to Heaven with me.

September 21, 1994
2:30 a.m.

Holy Is Thy Name

Holy is Thy name,
My precious Savior and King!
Holy is Thy name,
The Creator of everything!

Shout "Holy," all you people
Here on earth below.
Shout "Holy," all you heavenly hosts
Who wear the heavenly halo.

My Jesus is highly praised
Upon His throne above.
He is to be praised on earth
Because of His undying love.

He gave His life for us.
He gave it willingly
So that we could live with Him
Throughout eternity.

So *shout* "Holy," all you people;
In Heaven and on earth proclaim
Holiness to the Son of God,
For there *is* no other name

In Heaven or on earth
That is worthy to be praised.
Cry "Holy, hoiy, holy,"
As holy hands are raised.

September 27, 1994
1:15 a.m.

We Will Find God

NKJV, Proverbs 8:17 — I love those who love me, And those who seek me diligently will find me.

NKJV, Proverbs 8:35-36 — For whoever finds me finds life, and obtains favor from the Lord; But he who sins against me wrongs his own soul; All those who hate me love death.

The God of Heaven rains His love
On those who diligently seek Him.
He has promised, if they are sincere,
He will truly be found by them.

If we earnestly pray to God above
And we sincerely seek His face,
If we humbly come to Him in prayer,
What a glorious revelation of grace.

If we find God, we find life,
A life in Heaven with Him,
If we will only seek His face
And turn away from this life of sin.

We get so caught up in our own little world,
Thinking we need no one, but that is selfish pride.
Our way of life saddens Him so
When we leave our Father standing outside.

Remember to seek God each day when you wake
And seek Him ever so diligently.
Then you will find the greatest love you have ever known
And a life with Him throughout all eternity.

September 28, 1994
5:25 a.m.

The Lord of Hosts Is His Name

NKJV, Jeremiah 31:35 — Thus says the Lord, Who gives the sun for a light by day, the ordinances of the moon and the stars for a light by night, Who disturbs the sea, and its waves roar (The Lord of Hosts is His Name):

NKJV, Isaiah 51:15 — But I am the Lord your God, Who divided the sea whose waves roared — The Lord of hosts is His name.

Who put the sun in the sky?
The Lord of Hosts, I proclaim.
Who hung the moon and the stars?
The Lord of Hosts is His name.

Who made the rain and the snow
Come down from Heaven above?
Who blesses His own
And showers us with His love?

Who answers every prayer:
Where do we go? Whom do we seek?
To hear us when we pray
When we are so vile and weak?

Who is our joy
When sorrow engulfs us?
Who makes our hearts sing again
When trials get too tough?

Who comforts our hearts
When they are burdened with grief?
Where do we go
When we are desperate for relief?

Who holds us in His arms
When we feel so sad and alone?
Who whispers to our hearts
And lets us know we are His own?

The Lord of Hosts is His name.
Call to Him while He is near.
He will answer your every prayer,
And will take away all your fear.

October 2, 1994
1:00 a.m.

There Is No Limit with God

NKJV, Psalm 71:14-15—But I will hope continually, and I will praise You yet more and more. My mouth shall tell of Your righteousness and Your salvation all the day, for I do not know their limits.

Dear Father, I will continue
To praise You more and more each day,
My mouth shall tell of all Your righteousness,
For You give me the words to say.

Father, I will tell of Your salvation
And what it means to me.
I will witness of Your glory
And how you set my soul free.

Dear Jesus, I know there is no limit
To Your love, Your power, and Your glory.
That's why I love to praise You
And I love to tell the story,

The story of how You came to earth
To save sinners such as I.
And how You hung on that cruel tree;
How You were born to die.

Dear Jesus, just like You and Your limitless love
That You show continually for me,
I will keep witnessing and praising Your holy name
Through life and all eternity.

October 5, 1994
2:20 a.m.

You, Too, Will Suffer

NKJV, 2 Timothy 3:12 — Yes, and all who desire to live godly in Christ Jesus will suffer persecution.

Do you know that, when you live
Your life for Jesus each day,
You will suffer persecution
All along the way?

The world will look at you
Through their eyes, which cannot see,
Because they are blinded to the truth,
That Jesus can set them free.

When you are persecuted
For the way you live each day,
Remember Jesus, God's only Son,
And what He had to pay.

My Jesus gave His life
When He was nailed upon that tree to die.
He suffered such pain and torture
For sinners such as you and I.

He gave so much for us.
It was so sad to see
The humiliation and the hurt
When He hung upon that tree.

So, no matter how much you suffer,
Yes, you, too, will suffer if you live for Him.
Don't give up. It will be worth it.
Because He lives, you, too, will live again.

October 28, 1994
2:00 A.M.

No One but God

Who can paint a picture
Like the Lord on high
When He paints the trees
And the blue up in the sky?

He splashes color here
And He splashes color there.
No other artist
Can quite compare.

The reds, the greens,
The yellows so bright,
They all blend together.
What a beautiful sight!

How humble I feel
When my eyes do see
The magnificent picture
God has painted for me.

I realize how unworthy I am
Of God's beautiful love for me
When I gaze at the beauty of His world
In the color of the trees.

Mortal man cannot this picture paint.
All the beautiful, golden tones.
No one but God, Who created it all,
No one, but God alone.

(This poem was give to me while I was riding through the mountains
of North Carolina.)

October 28, 1994
10:00 a.m.

Are You a True Believer?

Are you a true believer?
Do you believe in Jesus, God's Son?
Do you believe in His Holy Word,
The Inspired Word? Yes! That's the One.

Do you pick it up
Each and every day?
Do you listen to His voice,
What His written words say?

Do you believe as you read
That these words are really true?
Do you think that they are meant
For everyone else but you?

Do you seek God's will
As you go through the pages of His Book?
Do you stop to pray and ask Him
Where He would have you look?

God's Word about the evil of this world
Is beginning to come to pass.
We can see it everyday;
Each day gets worse than the last.

Be a true believer.
Let others know where you stand.
Stand up for the Holy Book.
Keep hold of God's loving hand.

November 18, 1994,
11:10 a.m.

So Lost and Alone

NKJV, Psalm 10:4 — The wicked in his proud countenance does not seek God; God is in none of his thoughts.

There are people who live
Each and every day
Never seeking the Lord,
Trying to find their own way.

They never stop to think
About God or His Son.
They travel in darkness,
So lost and alone.

They go here and there
In a state of despair;
Not acknowledging that there is a God,
Not seeming to care.

I wonder what goes on
In their minds as they go
From one day to the next
In this sad state of woe.

Oh! If only they would wake up
And know that Jesus is there,
If they would humble themselves
And kneel down in prayer.

If they would call upon Him,
The One Who supplies every need,
If they would surrender their life to Him
And let Him take the lead,

Then what a wonderful peace
Would flood their soul.
No longer lost and alone,
For they would be made whole.

November 20, 1994
3:30 a.m.

He Shall Give His Angels Charge over You

NKJV, Psalm 91:9-11—Because you have made the LORD, who is my refuge, Even the Most High, your dwelling place, No evil shall befall you, Nor shall any plague come near your dwelling; For He shall give His angels charge over you, To keep you in all your ways.

Oh! What a glorious promise
That God has given to us,
To give His Holy angels charge.
How wonderful and how precious.

When you live for the Lord
And try to do your best,
When you wait upon His will
And in Him you rest,

He will give His angels
Charge over you.
No evil shall befall you
As this world you travel through.

What a comforting thought to know
That his angels are always near.
They are watching over us.
We are in no danger; never fear.

My God will always
Keep His loving hand on you.
Though you are down in a valley,
He is right there, down in the valley, too.

God will never leave us alone.
His angels are standing guard.
They will keep us safe from harm,
For He has given them charge.

November 24, 1994
2:00 a.m.

He Has Sealed Us

NKJV, 2 Corinthians 1:21-22—Now He who establishes us with you in Christ and has anointed us is God, who also has sealed us and given us the Spirit in our hearts as a guarantee.

NKJV, Ephesians 4:30—And do not grieve the Holy Spirit of God, by whom you were sealed for the day of redemption.

God has sealed His children
Unto the day of redemption
And has given us the Holy Spirit
As a deposit until our ascension.

He will live within our hearts
And will lead us through each day.
He will show us right from wrong
And will gently point the way.

Jesus died on the cross.
He took upon Himself our sins
So we could live forever
And reign forever with Him.

Just to know in my heart
That I have an eternal home;
To know I can live in his presence,
And I will never be alone,

That is the sweetest peace to me.
It is what I am longing for.
I know that I have been sealed
And will live forevermore.

November 29, 1994
11:30 p.m.

The True Church

NKJV, Ephesians 2: 19-22 — Now, therefore, you are no longer strangers and foreigners, but fellow citizens with the saints and members of the household of God, having been built on the foundation of the apostles and prophets, Jesus Christ Himself being the chief cornerstone, in whom the whole building, being fitted together, grows into a holy temple in the Lord, in whom you also are being built together for a dwelling place of God in the Spirit.

God is building His church,
The ones who are faithful and true,
The ones who live for Him
In obedience their whole life through.

There are those who are religious,
Who think that as long as they
Practice the form of church
Will inherit the Kingdom one day.

But this will not be the case.
Unless our faith is real,
Unless we walk with Jesus
And seek to do His will,

Unless we seek Him daily
And to Him humbly yield
Our lives in perfect submission
And are obedient to His will,

When He comes back one day
To take His true Church home,
The ones who are not sincere
Will be left without God or His Son.

Please get your life in order.
Make sure you are a part
Of the true Church of God.
Serve Him with all your heart.

December 3, 1994
4:50 a.m.

Worship the True God

Whom do you worship? Or is it what?
Do you worship God? Or have you forgot
That He is the One Who created all
And He is the One before whom you should fall

Down on your knees in worship and praise?
He is the One Who gives mercy and grace.
Kneel down before God, Who is Savior and King.
Let Him be your Lord, the Master of everything.

Worship the God Who was born that day
In a lowly manger filled with hay.
The God Who was born when the world could not find
A room for Him, not of any kind.

Worship the One Who was crucified,
Who died for you and me,
The One Who hung on the cross that day,
That day at Calvary.

Worship the God Who arose
From that grave in just three days,
The only One Who can give eternal life,
Who died that we could be saved.

Worship the real God,
The God of Heaven and earth.
He is the only God
Who can give us a new birth.

December 4, 1994
12:20 a.m.

I Believe

I believe, Dear Jesus,
That You are the Son of God.
I believe all of Your promises
That You give me in Your Word.

I believe that You came one day
As a tiny baby in Bethlehem.
I believe the reason that You came that way
Was to save me from all my sins.

I believe that, each time I kneel down in prayer
And I humbly seek Your holy face,
I believe You hear my every word,
No matter what time or what place.

I believe You went to that old rugged cross
And hung there upon that tree,
And, if I had been the only person on earth,
You still would have died for me.

I believe You are coming back one day
For me, for I am Your child.
I believe You will take me to Heaven with You,
And I believe it will be just a little while.

Dear Jesus, please help me to tell others
About You and Your wonderful plan.
Please make them realize that they are a part
And can go to that Heavenly land.

December 9, 1994
6:00 p.m.

A Child Is Born

NKJV, Isaiah 9:6—For unto us a Child is born, Unto us a Son is given; And the government will be upon His shoulder. And His name will be called Wonderful, Counselor, Mighty God, Everlasting Father, Prince of Peace.

One starry night in Bethlehem,
A beautiful Child is born.
He is the Son of the great I AM,
Our Savior and our Lord.

There was no great fanfare that night.
It was just a humble birth.
He came with no *big* ado.
He came to save this earth.

Behold this child
Who was born that day
And laid in a manger
On a bed of hay.

The beautiful star of Bethlehem
Shone so brightly over this child.
The shepherds and the wise men
Traveled for so many miles

Just to look on this beautiful face
Of the Savior, the new born King,
Just to worship at His feet
And to Him praises sing.

No one has ever been worthy enough
To merit this great love,
The love that the Father sent to us
When He sent His Son from Heaven above.

I love to praise this wonderful Child.
He is my Savior, you know,
The One that lives deep inside my heart,
The One Who is with me wherever I go.

December 10, 1994
8:00 a.m.

It Was All Written Down

NKJV, Psalm 139:16 — Your eyes saw my substance being yet unformed, And in Your book they all were written, The days fashioned for me, When as yet there were none of them.

Your eyes saw me.
In Your book I was found.
Before even I was born,
It was all written down.

You had my life all planned,
Each step I would take,
Each breath I would breathe,
For I am Your name's sake.

I was formed in Your image;
The likeness was to be the same.
That's the way I was made.
Oh, praise Your holy name!

I was made to follow your steps
And to learn to trust in You,
To humbly let You lead me
In everything I do.

I knew You would guide me
Each step that I took.
It was all written down
In the pages of Your Book.

December 11, 1994
4:00 a.m.

Wake Up, World

Wake up, world!
How long will it take?
Will Jesus return
Before you are awake?

His Word says to watch,
His vigilance to keep.
Don't let Him return
And find you asleep.

It's time that you get
Down on your knees and seek Him.
It's time to humble yourself
And turn from your life of sin.

When He comes back for His church,
It will be too late then.
You had better be ready
And be cleansed from within.

Although the time is known only
By the Father above
When He will send His Son
To gather up His beloved,

He will come swiftly,
As a thief in the night.
Make sure He will find you
With your light burning bright.

It's time to wake up, world.
Don't be asleep in your sins.
Make sure that, when He comes for you,
You will be ready and looking for Him.

December 15, 1994
6:30 p.m.

Whatever Comes

NKJV, Psalm 91: 4-6—He shall cover you with His feathers, And under His wings you shall take refuge; His truth shall be your shield and buckler. You shall not be afraid of the terror by night, Nor of the arrow that flies by day, Nor of the pestilence that walks in darkness, Nor of the destruction that lays waste at noonday.

Whatever comes our way each day,
Morning, noon, or night,
We do not have to be afraid
If we trust in Jesus with all our might.

Our God has promised us
That we can hide under His wings.
His mighty hand will keep us
Safe from everything.

Because we have made the Lord
Our refuge and our trust,
If we truly abide in His love,
No harm shall come to us.

Our God will not forsake us
Or ever leave us alone.
No matter what happens from day to day,
He protects us from upon His Throne.

He will be with us always,
In trouble and despair.
Whatever comes our way,
Our God is always there.

December 18, 1994
1:50 a.m.

The God of Heaven

NKJV, Revelation 22:4—They shall see His face, and His name shall be on their foreheads.

My Father, my God, my Savior, my Lord,
The God of Heaven is He.
He is the Maker, the almighty Creator,
He is Everything to me.

Holy, awesome, loving, and kind,
There is no other like He,
The God of Heaven, the Lord of all,
The Redeemer Who sets souls free.

He gives us wisdom to understand
His Holy Word as we read.
No matter how difficult it seems at times,
He always meets all of our needs.

The time will come
When we shall see His face,
When we get there
To that heavenly place.

We will stand in awe
And worship our King.
We will humbly bow
As His praises we will sing.

The God Of Heaven;
That is His name.
Every knee shall bow,
Every tongue will proclaim

That He is the Lord,
The Lord of everything.
Come worship Him with me,
The King of all kings.

December 22, 1994
10:30 a.m.

The Lord Will Never Forsake You

NKJV, Psalm 9:10—And those who know Your name will put their trust in You; For You, Lord, have not forsaken those who seek You.

If you trust in the Lord
With all of your heart,
If you seek His face,
He will never depart.

If you know His name
And upon Him you call,
He will never forsake you
When you stumble and fall.

You may feel so alone,
And you may be deep in despair,
But, if you are, look up! God is waiting;
He is always right there,

Patiently listening
For you to call out to Him.
He will always hear you
When your life seems so dark and dim.

While others about you
Are too busy to care,
Your troubles and your sorrows
He will always bear.

Our Lord is so good.
He is faithful and true.
Remember, when you seek Him,
He will never forsake you.

December 24, 1994
2:20 a.m.

Shadrach, Meshach, and Abed-Nego

NKJV, Daniel 3:25—"Look!" he answered, "I see four men loose, walking in the midst of the fire; and they are not hurt, and the form of the fourth is like the Son of God."

Nebuchadnezzar was a mean old king.
He thought his power was strong.
He ordered his people to worship
The idol all day long.

He made a certain rule
That, if they did not obey,
They would be thrown into
The fiery furnace that day.

There were these three men,
Shadrach, Meshach and Abed-Nego,
Who would not in any way worship
This graven image, oh, no!

This made the king so angry
He had the fire heated seven times more.
It was so hot that the men who took up these three
Were killed at the furnace door.

Shadrach, Meshach, and Abed-Nego
Were bound and thrown into the red hot flames,
But the next morning the king found them
Up walking, unhurt, and they were just the same.

This is not the end of the story.
There were not three, but four, up walking around.
The fourth man was the Son of God.
What a sight the king had found!

This goes to show us something:
That, if we always obey our God,
He will get right in there with us,
No matter where we have to trod

January 4, 1995
1:30 a.m.

Follow Me

NKJV, Matthew 4:19 — Then He said to them, "Follow Me, and I will make you fishers of men."

Jesus began to preach,
"Repent, for the Kingdom of Heaven is at hand."
He kept preaching this message
As He walked all over the land.

He saw two fishermen fishing.
Their names were Peter and Andrew.
Jesus said, "Follow Me,
And fishers of men I will make you."

They left their nets and followed Him.
And then He saw two more.
They were brothers, James and John,
In a boat not too far from shore.

They were mending their nets with their father
When Jesus called out to them.
They left their father and their boat
And immediately followed Him.

Now some others of the twelve were called,
And they followed Jesus with no fuss:
Philip, Bartholomew, Thomas,
Matthew, James, and Thaddaeus.

Simon was next to last to be called,
The last one being Judas.
He was the deceitful disciple
Who later betrayed our Lord Jesus.

These men did not hesitate
When Jesus called to them.
Wouldn't it be wonderful
If we were so quick to follow Him?

Jesus is calling all of us.
"Follow Me out of this world of sin.
Follow Me, and I will make you
All become fishers of men."

Dear Jesus, my Lord and Savior,
Lead me by Your loving, gentle hand.
I will follow You completely.
Please make me a fisher of men.

January 7, 1995
5:25 a.m.

The Great Love of God

NKJV, Romans 8:38-39—For I am persuaded that neither death nor life, nor angels nor principalities, nor powers, nor things present nor things to come, nor height nor depth, nor any other created thing, shall be able to separate us from the love of God which is in Christ Jesus our Lord.

The great love of God!
Oh, how awesome it is!
He showers it like raindrops
Upon us, This great love of His.

When you get so down and out
And sometimes feel so sad and blue,
Just pick up the Word of God
And let our God speak to you.

Whenever doubt comes,
And it sometimes does,
We need an uplift,
An assurance of God's love.

The Lord does not condemn us
When we are living for Him;
His great love fully engulfs us
As we turn away from sin.

Sometimes when I am weak
And know not how to pray,

The Holy Spirit living in me
Takes over and knows exactly what to say.

Our God above, who searches our hearts,
Knows the mind of the Spirit in us,
And the Spirit intercedes on our behalf,
Just as does our Lord Jesus.

There is no one or nothing
That can separate us from God's great love,
So, when you feel that you can't go on,
Just lift your eyes to the One above.

He can calm all your fears
And set your soul at rest,
For God's love is so great;
His love is the best.

January 7, 1995
9:00 a.m.

Taken for Granted

We oft times take for granted
The many blessings of God
As each day on our life's journey
We merrily trod along.

Until one day when something happens
Which puts us all out of whack.
Then we realize it is not us, but God,
Who keeps us on the right track.

I think God allows things to happen
To make us know that we
Could never carry our heavy load
Without almighty guidance from Thee.

There is not a single person
Who lives in this world of ours
Who doesn't need to be stopped now and then
Long enough to smell the flowers.

Please, God, don't ever let me again
Go about from day to day
And take for granted my life
Is in my hands in any way.

Let me always know I need You
To guide me each step that I take.
And, Father, I am so thankful
That you stopped me and got me awake.

January 9, 1995
12:25 p.m.

Delight Yourself in the Lord

NKJV, Psalm 37:3-5 — Trust in the LORD, and do good; Dwell in the land, and feed on His faithfulness. Delight yourself also in the Lord, and He shall give you the desires of your heart. Commit your way to the Lord, Trust also in Him, and He shall bring it to pass.

Delight yourself in the Lord,
And He shall give you the desires of your heart.
Commit your way unto Him,
And His blessing will surely start.

If you are totally committed
To His perfect will for you,
Just be patient and trust in Him,
And, in His time, His promises will all come true.

Be happy in the Lord
And wait upon Him.
Let Him have control of your life
And cleanse you of all your sin.

The Lord will give you your desires
If you will only trust in Him and do good,
If you will only live your life
Like His Word says you should.

Our God cannot be fooled;
He knows if you pretend.
You must seek Him sincerely, and then
Your desires will be fulfilled in the end.

January 15, 1995
12:00 a.m.

God Is Always There

NKJV, Psalm 139:7—Where can I go from Your Spirit? Or where can I flee from Your presence?

No matter where I am,
God is always there.
I can feel Him so near,
As near as a prayer.

When I awake in the morning,
When I open my eyes,
He is right there with me,
All my needs to supply.

When I walk down the street,
I know I'm not alone,
For my God is right there with me
Amid all of the throng.

When I sit down to eat,
I'm not ashamed for others to see
That I bow and thank God,
For He has given it to me.

When I lay down at night,
I can rest in His love,
For His peace is always with me,
For it comes from above.

It is so wonderful to feel
Such sweet peace and to know
That, no matter when or where,
God is with me wherever I go.

January 17, 1995
9:30 a.m.

How Wonderful Is Jesus

*NKJV, John 9:31—Now we know that God does not hear sinners;
but if anyone is a worshiper of God and does His will, He hears him.*

How wonderful is Jesus;
How wonderful is He.
He hung upon that cruel tree.
He hung there and died for me.

There is nothing I could ever do
To merit His great love.
I could never do anything
To earn a home above.

Isn't it so wonderful
That works do not get us there?
All we ever have to do
Is lift our voice in prayer.

All we need to do
Is to put our trust in Him,
To follow wherever He leads us
And then feel that sweet peace come in.

How wonderful is Jesus.
My Savior, my God, is He.
If, by faith, I do His Holy will,
My burdens He will set free.

February 9, 1995
3:00 a.m.

Stand the Test

NKJV, James 1:12—Blessed is the man who endures temptation; for when he has been approved, he will receive the crown of life which the Lord has promised to those who love Him.

There are times in our lives
When God puts us to the test.
If we only do His holy will,
He will do the rest.

What He asks us to bear
Seems oft times too hard to do,
But if we will only trust Him
He will always carry us through.

His Holy Book tells us
He will never ask me or you
To stand any test too hard for us,
For He will give us strength to see it through.

No matter how difficult it may seem,
The test we are asked to bear,
We need never fear; we are not alone,
For my Jesus will always be right there.

Dear Jesus, I thank You for carrying me
Safely through each valley I face,
For I know I will receive the crown of life
Because of Your mercy and Your grace.

February 15, 1995
10:45 a.m.

King Jesus

All Hail, King Jesus!
The King of *all* kings,
My Lord and my Master,
How He makes my heart sing.

He is worthy to be called
King Jesus, don't you see?
For He gave His all for me.
Let me hide myself in Thee.

His blood He shed
To cover all my sins.
He gave it so willingly.
How I praise and worship Him.

He has given me such a sweet peace
That no one or nothing could ever do.
When I gave Him control of my life,
His Light came shining through.

King Jesus will reign
Throughout all eternity
Upon His glorious throne
For you and for me.

Don't go around with a long, sad face.
When He is holding out His hand to you,
Just reach up as He is reaching down.
Let King Jesus put this peace in your heart, too.

February 20, 1995
12:20 a.m.

In the Shadow of Your Wings

NKJV, Psalm 63:7—Because You have been my help, Therefore in the shadow of Your wings I will rejoice.

In the shadow of Your wings
I will rejoice.
I will lift my hands to You,
And I will lift my voice.

I will put my trust in You.
I will never be ashamed
To lift holy hands
And praise Your dear name.

I will bow down before You
And let the whole world see
That You are my Lord.
You mean everything to me.

You are my refuge.
I can come to You.
When my road gets too rough,
You will always carry me through.

I know You will hear
When I lift my voice in prayer.
I need never worry,
For You will always be there

To lead and to guide me.
Your praises I will sing.
I know You will keep me forever
In the shadow of Your wings.

(I love you, Jesus.)

February 20, 1995
2:10 a.m.

Well Done, My Child

"Well done, My child,"
Is what I want to hear Him say
When I stand before Him
On that Great Judgment Day.

Everything will be worth it,
All the troubles and the trials
That I faced while on this earth,
Just to see His beautiful smile,

Just to see His arms outstretched,
Beckoning me to come to Him,
Just to know I've made it home
And the King of kings is welcoming me in.

I want to kneel down at His feet.
I want to praise My Father above.
I want to thank Him face-to-face
For His wonderful, unconditional love.

Dear Father, I just want to thank You
For those words you will say to Your own
That wonderful day, not far away,
When we stand before Your throne.

February 22, 1995
4:20 p.m.

Wisdom

NKJV, Job 38:36 — Who has put wisdom in the mind? Or who has given understanding to the heart?

Dear Lord, I pray
As I seek You today
For the wisdom to help others
As we go along our way.

I know I am not smart;
I never pretended to be.
All the wisdom I have
Comes completely from Thee.

Your Holy Word tells us
If we want wisdom to ask.
You will supply more than we need
To complete any task.

There are those who are searching
For meaning in their life.
Please help me to help them
Through their troubles and strife.

Let them see, Dear Lord,
That *all* wisdom comes from You.
All they need to do is ask;
You will always carry them through.

Father, please let Your Light
Shine brightly through me.
Please give me wisdom
To witness for Thee.

February 28, 1995
7:50 a.m.

God's Sweet Holy Spirit

NKJV, 1 Corinthians 2:12—Now we have received, not the spirit of the world, but the Spirit who is from God, that we might know the things that have been freely given to us by God.

Jesus died upon the cross
To save the lost from sin.
He was buried in an empty tomb,
And then He arose again.

He was raised from that tomb
In just three short days,
Then He ascended to Heaven to sit,
At the Father's right hand to stay.

But He didn't leave us all alone.
He made provisions for us from above,
For He sent His sweet Holy Spirit
To lead us in His love.

His sweet Holy Spirit came to abide
Deep down inside the hearts of men.
He speaks to us with His gentle voice
As He cleanses us from all sin.

What a sweet, sweet and wonderful peace
His presence to behold
As He gently and softly speaks to me
And His blessings He unfolds.

Thank You, Dear Jesus, for Your guiding hand
That will never, never depart.
Thank You for Your sweet, sweet Holy Spirit
That lives deep down in my heart.

March 6, 1995
12:30 a.m.

Draw Near to God

NKJV, Psalm 73:28—But it is good for me to draw near to God; I have put my trust in the Lord God, That I may declare all Your works.

It is good for us
To draw near to God.
It is good for us to seek Him
In His Holy Word.

His Holy Word tells us
He has to draw us to Him.
He will deliver us
From the depths of our sins.

No matter how low
We have let ourselves get,
There is but one sin bad enough
That He will not forget.

The sin that is bad enough
For Him not to forgive or forget
Is to sin against Him
If you blaspheme His Holy Spirit.

I have put my trust
In the Lord God above;
I will declare all His works
And His wonderful, agape love.

Don't wait until it's too late,
Until He gives up on you.
Repent of your sins.
Ask Him into your heart, too.

Draw near to God.
Let Him guide Your way.
He is waiting for you.
Please call out to Him today.

March 9, 1995
2:35 a.m.

My Walk with God

My desire each day is to walk with God,
To let Him completely lead my way.
I seek His presence to guide me along
Lest my footsteps falter and sway.

My walk would be so crooked and rough;
I could never make it alone.
He is my wisdom; my strength is He.
I need His hand to gently lead me along.

I would be so lonesome if I couldn't feel Him there,
His sweet, gentle hand holding mine,
The tug at my heart as He speaks to me.
My Jesus, so loving and kind.

I just don't understand how some cannot see
How much easier and sweeter life could be
If they would walk each day with my God, so sweet,
As they surrender their life to Thee.

My walk with God, what a beautiful walk,
For I know I am never alone,
And I know if I keep holding tight to His hand
He will lead me all the way home.

March 12, 1995
3:45 a.m.

Paul and Silas

NKJV, Acts 16: 30-31 — And he brought them out and said, "Sirs, What must I do to be saved?" So they said, "Believe on the Lord Jesus Christ, and you will be saved, you and your household."

Paul and Silas were in prison;
They were both locked up tight.
They were singing and praising their God.
It was late: twelve o'clock midnight.

Suddenly there came this earthquake.
As always, their God was right there.
The prison doors flew open;
The cells *could have* become bare.

The keeper of the prison came running;
He supposed that the prisoners had fled.
He drew his sword toward himself;
In a moment he would have been dead.

But Paul called out with a loud voice,
"We are here, do yourself no harm."
The guard got a light and came running;
He was filled with so much alarm,

He fell down at the feet of Paul and Silas.
He said, "Sirs, what must I do to be saved?"
They said, "Believe on the Lord Jesus Christ;
You *and* your household will be saved."

What a wonderful and awesome God we serve.
He gives so much mercy and grace.
I will worship and praise Him forever,
And someday I shall see Him face to face.

March 13, 1995
12:15 a.m.

Through Christ

NKJV, Philippians 4:13—I can do all things through Christ Who strengthens me.

Nothing is too difficult,
No matter how much the fuss,
If we open our hearts to Christ
And let Him work through us.

When we arise in the morning,
If we will seek His holy face,
We will find there is no other
Who can give us His wonderful grace.

He is our source and strength;
He fills us with His love.
He leads and guides our footsteps
As He looks down on us from above.

If we keep our eyes on Jesus,
Not looking from side to side,
Our road will be less rocky.
How much smoother will be the ride

Learn to depend on Jesus;
Learn to trust in Him.
Life will be so much sweeter
As His sweet peace moves right in.

He is so awesome and mighty;
He is my God and King.
Through Christ, my Blessed Redeemer,
Through His strength, I can do all things.

March 18, 1995
5:20 a.m.

If You Walk with God

NKJV, Isaiah 41:10 — Fear not, for I am with you; Be not dismayed, for I am your God. I will strengthen you, Yes, I will help you, I will uphold you with My righteous right hand.

If you walk with God,
He promises that you
Do not have to fear.
He will lead you safely through.

No matter how rough
Or how rocky your road,
His gentle, loving hand
Will always ease your heavy load.

He tells us not to be dismayed;
His strength He will give to us,
For He is our God.
All we need to do is trust.

He promises that He
Will always be there.
He will never leave us.
He is no further than a prayer.

Your crooked places He will make straight,
No matter how far you trod.
Life is so much sweeter
If you seek and walk with God.

March 18, 1995
11:20 p.m.

Salvation Is Eternal

NKJV, Isaiah 51:6 — Lift up your eyes to the heavens, And look on the earth beneath. For the heavens will vanish away like smoke, The earth will grow old like a garment, And those who dwell in it will die in like manner; But My salvation will be forever, And My righteousness will not be abolished.

No one can take away
The salvation of the Lord.
No one can take away
The power of His Word.

Lift up your eyes to Heaven
And look on the earth below.
See the mighty works of God;
See the beauty His hands did bestow.

Heaven and earth were created,
But they shall pass away.
There will be a new Heaven
And a new earth one beautiful day.

But salvation is eternal.
Jesus died for us upon the cross
To give us a brand new life,
To save and redeem the lost.

God tells us in His Word;
Jesus preached It all over the land.

There is nothing and there is no one
Who can pluck us out of His hand.

What a wonderful, blessed assurance,
When Jesus lives deep down in your heart,
To know that salvation is eternal
And from us He will never depart.

March 31, 1995
2:40 a.m.

In the Midnight Hours

In the midnight hours
When the world is asleep,
Let me feel Your presence, Lord.
Oh! How beautiful and how sweet.

Let me watch and pray.
Draw me closer to You.
Feed my soul with Your Presence
All the night through.

Oh, how soft is the stillness
When there's just You and I.
What sweet fellowship together
As the minutes go by.

To read Your Word, Lord,
To hide it in my heart,
To lift praises to You
Until the teardrops start,

To commune with You
There in the night,
To feel the beauty
Of the Everlasting Light.

In the midnight hours
While the house is asleep,
Reach down and touch us, Lord,
And my family, please keep.

April 2, 1995
12:00 a.m.

It's Me Again, Lord

NKJV, Psalm 37:3 — Trust in the Lord, and do good; Dwell in the land, and feed on His faithfulness.

It's me again, Lord,
Calling out to You.
Please hear my humble prayer;
Please let it get through.

Down here on my knees
As I lift my voice in prayer,
Please let me feel Your presence;
Please let me know You are there.

Please feel me with trust,
And give me more faith, too.
Let me be the Christian
That is pleasing to You.

I want more of You, Lord,
From my head to my toes.
Please make me more like You,
And let the world know

That I am Your child
And I am living for You.
Let them see Jesus in me;
Let *You* come shining through.

It's me again, Lord,
I need to feel Your touch.
I just want to tell You
That I love You so very much.

April 22, 1995
1:30 p.m.

This Kind of Faith

Acts 3

Peter and John were going
Up to the temple to pray.
There they saw a crippled man;
At the gate of the temple he lay.

He was just a humble beggar;
That was all that he could do
Because he had been crippled from birth,
Could not walk his whole life through.

Then he saw Peter and John,
And he begged alms from them.
They gazed at him intently,
And this is what Peter said to him:

"Silver and gold have I none,
But what I have I give to thee
In the name of Jesus Christ of Nazareth
Walk!" And they helped him to his feet immediately.

He went walking and leaping and praising God;
Into the temple he went with them.
The people who saw him were so amazed
At what had happened to him.

Then Peter seeing, all their surprise,
Let them know, and it didn't take long.
It was not them but by faith and in Jesus' name
That had made this man well and strong.

Dear Friend, if you can have this kind of faith,
Just call out to the Father in Jesus' name.
By faith, you, too, can be healed,
And your life will never be the same.

You, too, will go walking and leaping and praising God
And witnessing to everyone you see.
There's nothing as good as the peace of God.
When He lives in your heart, He sets you free.

April 22, 1995
11:30 p.m.

My Daughter, Rest in Me

NKJV, Psalm 37:7-9 — Rest in the LORD, and wait patiently for Him; Do not fret because of him who prospers in his way, Because f the man who brings wicked schemes to pass. Cease from anger, and forsake wrath; Do not fret — it only causes harm. For evildoers shall be cut off; But those who wait on the LORD, They shall inherit the earth.

Lord, sometimes I feel so lonely,
So far away from You.
It seems I'm out there wandering,
Not knowing what to do.

I get so upset and worried.
I think, Now where is He?
At times like these, You tell me,
"My Daughter, rest in Me."

You tell me to be patient,
To humbly wait for You.
Why can't I just trust You
To safely lead me through

Each trial and each sorrow
As down each path I trod?
Lord, help me always remember
That You are Almighty God.

Let all my doubts disappear.
Let me go in the strength of Thee
When You whisper gently in my heart,
"My Daughter, rest in me."

May 4, 1995
12:15 a.m.

Show Me Your Path for Me

NKJV, Isaiah 2:3 – Many people shall come and say, "Come, and let us go up to the mountain of the Lord, To the house of the God of Jacob; He will teach us His ways, And we shall walk in His paths."

Dear Lord, as I kneel
Humbly down on my knees,
I ask You to show me
Your path for me.

I cannot find my way
In this world on my own.
I want to walk the path
That leads straight to Your throne.

When I try to walk
Without seeking Your will,
My path seems to be headed
Straight up every steep hill.

Your path for me
Is smooth and straight.
It will lead and guide me
Straight to Heaven's pearly gate.

I love You, dear Jesus,
And I want to please You.
Please show me each day
What You would have me do.

Teach me Your way, Lord.
Let me walk daily with Thee.
Please show me Your path
That You have laid out for me.

May 24, 1995
5:00 a.m.

Come, Let Us Worship

NKJV, Psalm 95:6—Oh come, let us worship and bow down; Let us kneel before the LORD our Maker. For He is our God, And we are the people of His pasture, And the sheep of His hand....

Oh come, let us worship.
Let us bow down before Him,
For He is our God.
He will forgive all our sins.

If we kneel down before Him
And call out His name,
He will enter our hearts,
And we will never be the same.

Oh, worship the Lord,
Ye people of all lands!
Reach up to find Him.
He is reaching down His hand.

Praise Him! Glorify His name!
For He is the King of all kings.
Bow down before His Throne.
Let Him be Lord of everything.

He is the only answer
To the turmoil within.
Just call on Him today,
And feel His sweet peace come in.

You will never know
How peaceful and sweet
Your life can become
Until you kneel at His feet.

Listen! He is calling out to you.
Can't you hear His sweet voice?
Let go and let God.
How your soul will rejoice.

May 25, 1995
8:15 a.m.

Mary

NKJV, Luke 1:46-49—And Mary said: "My soul magnifies the Lord, And my spirit has rejoiced in God my Savior. For He has regarded the lowly state of His maidservant; For behold, henceforth all generations will call me blessed. For He who is mighty has done great things for me, And holy is His name."

Mary was the chosen one
From all the women on earth
To be called blessed
And to give a virgin birth.

She was the one
That God had chosen to be
The mother of His Son,
Who would come to set men free.

She was only a maidservant,
So humble and so low,
When God sent His angel,
Good news upon her to bestow.

She could hardly believe it
When the angel came and said,
"Mary, you are chosen,"
And by the Spirit she was led.

Mary was a wonderful mother;
She nursed and cared for God's Son.
She magnified and worshiped Him,
For He is the Holy One.

May 31, 1995
12:50 a.m.

Prayer Changes Things

No matter what the problem,
No matter how bad the pain,
Just turn it over to Jesus.
He will fix it again and again.

My Jesus, He is so loving,
So gentle and so kind.
Your prayers He will always answer,
And His peace you will always find.

Don't think you are all alone,
No matter how lost you feel.
Just call out to my Savior;
He will hear you if you will.

He is so good and so understanding;
He is always standing by
To hear you when you call Him
Our Father, up on High.

Prayer always changes things.
Remember, your problems He can solve.
Just trust and call out to Jesus;
Let Him answer you with His love.

June 21, 1995
11:00 a.m.

Call Upon Me

NKJV, Psalm 50:15—Call upon Me in the day of trouble; I will deliver you, and you shall glorify Me.

"Call upon Me,"
Says the Lord above,
"When you are troubled,
I will give you love.

I will deliver you
From the fiery darts;
I will give you peace
Deep down in your heart.

When you feel My touch
And my love you see,
When your troubles are gone,
You shall glorify Me.

I love you, My child,
And I long to be
Your source of strength
To set your soul free.

So call upon Me.
Let Me be your stay.
Call upon Me.
I will answer you today."

July 3, 1995
7:00 a.m.

Christ Living in You

NKJV, Galatians 2:20—I have been crucified with Christ; it is no longer I who live, but Christ lives in me; and the life which I now live in the flesh I live by faith in the Son of God, who loved me and gave Himself for me.

When you are saved,
It is no longer you who lives.
You are crucified with Christ
When your salvation He gives.

It is no longer you who lives,
But it is Christ Who lives in you,
For the old man Is gone;
Your soul has been made new.

When you ask Lord Jesus
To come into your heart,
You are dead to your old life,
And your new life will start.

You will live by faith
And not by sight
Until Jesus returns
And you take your Heavenly flight.

Ask Him today to save you.
Don't be afraid; *be bold.*
Give your heart to Jesus;
He will save your soul.

July 4, 1995
12:15 a.m.

When I Am Weak, You Are Strong

When I am weak,
You are strong.
I lean on you
All the day long.

You give me strength
Along my way.
I seek Your face at the start
Of each new day.

I could not travel
This life alone.
I need You to hear
And to guide me home.

What do people do
When they don't have You
In their lives each day
To gently guide them through?

How alone I would be
As each day moves along?
Because, when I am weak,
Then You are strong.

July 5, 1995
7:40 a.m.

God Is my Light

NKJV, Psalm 27: 1—The Lord is my light and my salvation; Whom shall I fear? The Lord is the strength of my life; Of whom shall I be afraid?

When my world falls around me
And my life seems dark and drear,
I will turn my eyes toward Heaven,
For my God is always near.

He is my light, my beacon,
My salvation; I need not fear.
He is the strength of my life.
When I call out, He will hear.

When life's problems get too heavy
And it seems I can't go on,
There is Someone close beside me;
I will never be alone.

God has promised in times of trouble
He will see me safely through.
If you also truly seek Him,
He will draw so close to you.

My God is my light
In the darkness. When it comes,
I will look to Him for comfort
And let Him safely guide me home.

July 24, 1995
1:15 a.m.

We Shall Arise

NKJV, Isaiah 26:19 — Your dead shall live; Together with my dead body they shall arise. Awake and sing, you who dwell in dust; For your dew is like the dew of herbs, And the earth shall cast out the dead.

NKJV, Daniel 12:13 — But you, go your way till the end; for you shall rest, and will arise to your inheritance at the end of the days.

Thank You, Dear Jesus,
That, because You live,
A new body like You
To us You will give.

One day we shall arise.
We shall awake and sing.
We shall live with You.
Let Heaven's joy bells ring!

The ones who have lived
And walked with Him,
The ones who have prayed
And repented of their sins,

Shall arise to meet Jesus
And go home with Him that day
To live in sweet peace,
For all eternity to stay.

Ask Him to forgive
All the bad you have done,
And one day you shall arise
And go to your new home.

August 17, 1995
1:00 a.m.

Be Ready

When Jesus returns
From His home on High,
When the clouds roll back
Up there in the sky,

When we see him descend
From Heaven to earth
To call the redeemed
Who have received the new birth,

Will you be ready?
Will your robe be white?
Will you be ready to meet Him,
Be it day or night?

Now is the time.
Don't wait until it's too late.
Be ready to enter
Heaven's pearly gate.

Don't miss it with God;
Seek salvation today.
Be washed in Jesus' blood.
Be ready, I pray.

August 27, 1995
1:00 a.m.

You, Too, Can Be Saved

NKJV, Romans 10:9 — that if you confess with your mouth the Lord Jesus and believe in your heart that God has raised Him from the dead, you will be saved.

It's not by works so we can boast
That Jesus saves from sin.
It's not by anything we do;
It's total faith in Him.

God's Word is written very clear;
He plainly spells it out.
We can surely all be saved,
That's true, without a doubt.

We must confess with our mouth
That Jesus Christ is Lord.
We must believe with all our heart
Everything written in God's Word.

We must believe that Jesus died
Upon that rugged cross.
We must believe God raised His Son,
His blood to save the lost.

Dear Jesus, I confess to all.
You are God's precious Son.
I believe You would have been raised
Had I been the only one.

But I know that God raised You,
And it was not only for me.
You died to show God's love for us
So that everyone could see

His perfect plan that was arranged
Before this world began,
That You would come, die, and be raised
To save the soul of man.

So, lost person, you out there,
You, too, can be saved from sin.
Confess with your mouth and believe with your heart
And live forever in Heaven with Him.

August 30, 1995
10:00 a.m.

Forever Stay Close to Me

Dear Lord, You've seemed so far away;
I know the fault is mine.
No matter how far away you've seemed,
You were near me all the time.

It's me who strayed away from You;
I didn't constantly seek Your face.
I didn't spend enough time in Your Word;
I let other things take Your place.

Oh, Lord, my God, I humbly bow
Down on my knees in shame.
I ask for mercy; I ask for grace.
I ask in Jesus' name.

Dear God, I know You will hear me
If I come through Jesus, Your Son.
I know You will forgive me
Because this you have already done.

You died to take my sins away.
You died to set me free.
And so, Dear Lord, please forgive me
And forever stay close to me.

October 2, 1995
12:50 a.m.

I Asked, You Gave

Dear Lord, as I knelt
Down on my knees
And as I prayed,
You heard my pleas.

As I cried,
Joy came flooding back.
It filled my heart,
The joy I lacked.

Dear Lord, I know
All I have to do
Is to seek Your face,
And You will show me *You*.

When I kneel and pray,
You will hear my prayer.
When I call out to You,
You will always be there.

Thank You, dear Lord,
That, once again,
I feel so close to You.
You are my best friend.

October 2, 1995
4:00 a.m.

Who May Live with Jesus?

NKJV, Psalm 24: 3-4 — Who may ascend into the hill of the LORD? Or who may stand in His holy place? He who has clean hands and a pure heart, Who has not lifted up his soul to an idol, Nor sworn deceitfully.

Who may live with Jesus
In that heavenly home one day?
Who is He coming back for,
In His presence forever to stay?

Is it the one who has lived his own way
In his own world filled with sin,
The one who has walked in darkness
And put everything else before Him?

Who may stand in His holy place
One day around His great throne?
Who is He coming back for
To take to His heavenly home?

He who has clean hands
And the one whose heart is pure,
Who has not put other things before Him,
Who will be ready and looking, for sure!

Make sure your hands are clean
And make sure your heart is right.
Live your life pure and holy
And be looking, day and night.

Jesus *is* coming back real soon.
Will you be ready? Will He find
Your wedding gown all spotless?
Be Ready! Don't be left behind!

October 8, 1995
3:40 a.m.

O Lord, Our Lord

NKJV, Psalm 8:1 — O Lord, our Lord, How excellent is Your name in all the earth, Who have set Your glory above the heavens!

O Lord, our Lord,
How excellent is Your name in all the earth.
The One Who was sacrificed, Who died
To give us a second birth,

We magnify, we glorify,
We praise Your holy name.
When we give our hearts to You, O Lord,
We will never be the same.

The name above all names, O Lord,
We lift our hearts in praise.
The Holy One, the omnipotent Son
Who died and then was raised.

How wonderful are Your works, O Lord.
None other can compare.
The moon, the sun, the earth, O Lord,
You spoke, and they were there.

You have a mighty plan, O Lord,
For all who walk with You.
It will unfold in Your time, Lord.
We know It will come true.

And so we wait, O Lord, for You,
And praise You, O most high.
O Lord, our Lord, how wonderful it will be
To meet You in the sky.

November 4, 1995
4:25 a.m.

Almighty God

*NKJV, Jeremiah 32:17—Ah, L*ord *God! Behold, You have made the heavens and the earth by Your great power and outstretched arm. There is nothing too hard for You.*

Oh, great and mighty God,
The almighty God of Heaven and earth,
Thou Who created us
And died to give us a new birth,

No matter how difficult
Our problems seem to be,
We need never have a fear
When we draw near to Thee.

When problems arise,
And they so often do,
We can turn to the problem solver,
And that, Lord Jesus, is You.

There is never one problem
Too difficult for Thee.
I know You will always
Solve my problems for me.

Oh, if everyone would realize
You are all that they need,
If they would turn to You,
By Your Holy Spirit, You would lead.

Their problems would vanish
Like the smoke in the sky
If they would give them to You,
Almighty God up on high.

November 9, 1995
2:00 a.m.

God's Child Is Born

NKJV, Isaiah 7:14—Therefore the Lord Himself will give you a sign; Behold, the virgin shall conceive and bear a Son, and shall call His name Immanuel.

NKJV, Isaiah 9:6—For unto us a Child is born, Unto us a Son is given; And the government will be upon His shoulder. And His name will be called Wonderful, Counselor, Mighty God. Everlasting Father, Prince of Peace.

A tiny Babe was born
That night in Bethlehem.
He came to save the world,
To cleanse us all from sin.

He was laid that night
In a manger bed of hay.
The reason that He came
Was to show us a better way.

Our Father up in Heaven
Had a great master plan;
He planned to redeem and save
The soul of every man.

The tiny Babe Who came
Was the holy Son of God.
He came in the form of man
Upon this world to trod.

He walked as you and me.
He was the perfect man.
He preached and healed the sick
As He witnessed all over the land.

Oh, what a master plan
The Lord has laid out for us!
Through the precious blood
Of His only Son, Jesus,

He says we, too, can have
The power He gave His Son
If we submit to His Spirit
Through Jesus, the Holy One.

November 27, 1995
4:10 a.m.

The City Built Four-Square

I've read in God's Word
About a city built four-square,
Such a beautiful city;
There's none to compare.

Its walls are of jasper,
Its streets paved with gold.
It's a city so beautiful
Where we will never grow old.

Our loved ones will be waiting
To greet us at the gates,
But Jesus' sweet face
I long to see. I can't wait.

He has promised to wipe
Every tear from our eyes,
And the love that we'll feel
Will be no surprise,

For His Holy Word tells us
That Jesus *is* love.
He'll surround us with beauty
In our home up above.

Come quickly, Lord Jesus!
Take us home with You there,
To that beautiful city,
The city built four-square.

June 20, 1996
8:30 a.m.

If Today Were the Day

If I knew that for certain
Today would be the day
When I would go to Heaven
With my Jesus to stay,

The most important task
That I feel led to do
Would be to talk about how
You can go to Heaven, too.

I wouldn't be afraid;
I would be so bold.
I would come straight out and ask
About the condition of your soul.

You see, sometimes we think
Our lives are as they should be,
But the truth is our eyes are scaled
And it is difficult to see.

We need to ask God
To remove the scales from our eyes
So when that Day comes
There will be no surprise.

We don't know how long
Before Jesus will come
To gather up His children
And take them all Home.

Please examine your life.
Pray to Jesus above.
Let Him show you His mercy;
Let Him show you His love.

Ask Him to show you
If you are all right with Him;
Ask Him to show you
If you are cleansed within.

How beautiful our home
In Heaven must be.
I can hardly wait
My Jesus to see.

Please ask Jesus into your heart.
Get reborn and free.
Get your life in order,
And go home with me.

November 9, 2004

God Speaks to Me Through Butterflies

God speaks to us in many ways
If only we will listen for Him.
We have to open up our hearts
And let His sweet Voice come in.

He speaks to me through butterflies,
Which may seem strange to you,
But I know that He is speaking
When His Presence I can feel so true.

He gave me a beautiful dream, you see,
On a summer's night many years ago.
It was about a butterfly
With vivid colors all aglow.

I had heard many years before
That you would be in a tunnel when you die.
Well, all of a sudden I was in this tunnel
Sailing upward toward the sky.

I was headed straight toward the butterfly,
The most beautiful I had ever seen.
When I reached it, I went straight through it.
I awoke with a peace so serene.

I felt I had landed in Heaven,
And I could hear God speaking to me.
He told me that one day I would be with Him
To live for eternity.

Now you can see why I feel such joy
And why my heart feels happy and free,
And now you can see why I say what I do,
That God speaks through butterflies to me.

February 2, 2002

I Love You, Dear Lord

I love You, dear Lord
And I now understand
That Yours is the sweetest love
In all of the land.

Even in the valleys,
Where I sometimes have to go,
You are always there with me
With Your love all aglow.

You are my strength,
The real meaning of life.
You always calm my fears
Amid all of my strife.

Some days I feel
That I'm really put to the test,
But I try to do my best,
And You always do the rest.

You are such a good God.
I wish everyone could see
That a relationship with You
Is *as good* as life can be.

July 23, 2002

God Will Gather His Sheep

He was in the beginning;
All things were made by Him.
He came down from the Father
To save this world from sin.

He was born of a virgin;
He was God's only Son.
He came not only for me,
But He came for everyone.

His Name is Jesus,
A name filled with love.
He came straight from Heaven,
Straight from God above.

He came to bring us peace
And rest for our weary soul.
If one of His sheep goes astray,
He will bring it back into His fold.

One day He's coming back.
His sheep He will gather in.
He'll take us up to Heaven
To live forever with Him.

November 21, 2002
2:20 a.m.

Will You Let Me Tell You?

Will you let me tell you?
The greatest thing I can do for you
Is to tell you what God's Word says
In the Bible, which is ever so true.

I cannot keep secret the message
I must tell you about the One
With Whom you can live forever.
He's Jesus, God's Holy Son.

Our Blessed Lord and Savior
Died while He hung on the rugged cross.
But, bless the name of Jesus,
He arose to save all the lost.

I know some people don't believe this,
That Jesus arose from the dead.
They think He's still in that dark tomb
And will arise another day instead.

Praise God! He arose on the third day,
And He walked the earth for forty more,
Then He ascended to Heaven
To wait for His children on Heaven's shore.

He gave us a mission: to tell others
How they can live forever with Him.
They have to realize and confess it:
That they are living in sin.

And when they call upon Jesus
To deliver and save their soul,
He will hear from His throne in Heaven
And will bring them into the fold.

There we'll all live together
Throughout all eternity,
For our Lord has made us a promise
That we'll all be a family.

So you see why I must tell you
Before it's eternally too late,
Because God gave me a mission,
And I'll be waiting for you at the gate.

March 10, 2003

Overcoming Temptation

NKJV, Luke 4:1-2—Then Jesus, being filled with the Holy Spirit, returned from the Jordan and was led by the Spirit into the wilderness, being tempted for forty days by the devil. And in those days He ate nothing, and afterward, when they had ended, He was hungry.

Jesus was led into the desert
By the Holy Spirit one day.
Satan appeared before Him,
And this was what He had to say:

"If You are the Son of God,
Make bread from this stone."
Jesus replied to Satan,
"Man does not live by bread alone."

Satan then led Him to a high place,
Splendor as far as they could see.
Satan said, "It will all be Yours
If You will worship me."

Jesus then told Satan, "It is written."
And He quoted the Scripture to him:
"Worship the Lord Your God,
And serve only Him."

Then Satan led Jesus to Jerusalem,
And there, on the highest hill,

He told Jesus if He was the Son of God
To throw Himself down, but still

Jesus quoted more Scripture.
"Do not put the Lord Your God to the test."
At these words, Satan left Him.
I'm sure Satan needed a rest.

Oh, how awesome our God is!
He was tempted by Satan forty days.
Jesus knew Scripture was the *weapon*,
So He quoted it all along the way.

We can use Jesus' example
When tempted by Satan each day.
Just simply quote the scripture
And humbly bow your head and pray.

March 20, 2003

Life Without God Is Senseless

Life without God is senseless.
Why can't everyone see?
That to try life without Him...
Oh, what a catastrophe!

God the Father, Jesus, the Son, and the Holy Spirit
Make up the Holy Trinity.
They have come to show us
Their great love for you and me.

God the Father looks down from Heaven
With Jesus, His Son, at His right side.
The Holy Spirit dwells within us
If we're saved, our walk to guide.

He knows every step we take
From morning until night.
Before we even take them,
They are already in His sight.

Please know that life without God is senseless;
Please accept Jesus into your heart;
Please let the Blessed Holy Spirit
Abide with you, never to depart.

June 10, 2003

God Has the Last Word

We may plan in our heart
The path we will take,
But the way of our steps
Our holy God will make.

It may seem right to us
When we make our plans,
But the Plan has already been made
By the Son of Man.

From the break of the morn
Until the setting of the sun,
Our steps are ordered
By the great Holy One.

So remember today,
When you plan your way,
That our great God above
Will have the last say.

January 28, 2004

Little by Little

NKJV, Matthew 19:14—But Jesus said, "Let the little children come to Me, and do not forbid them; for of such is the kingdom of heaven.

Little by little,
Christ-like we become.
We have to start with baby steps
To become like Jesus, God's Son.

We have to be taught,
And we have to be led.
We have to open the Word,
And by it we are fed.

When we came into this world,
We came as a tiny child.
We had to be taught
Because we were so tender and mild.

And God says that we must
Come to Him as a child.
Little by little, our efforts
Will be worth the while.

We will reach God's throne
If in humility we pray
And come as a child
Each and every day.

January 29, 2004

I'm Going Up to Heaven

I'm going up to Heaven
To live with Jesus one day.
I hope you will go with me,
And for this each day I pray.

Jesus went on before us
When He arose from the grave
To prepare a place for us,
For all who have been saved.

His Father made a plan, and
We are included in His plan.
Jesus will come back one day for us.
I hope you understand.

We need to call upon Him
To send His Spirit within.
Each and every one of us
Needs to be cleansed from our sin.

He has promised to take us with Him
To that mansion in the sky,
So be sure and be ready
When He comes for you and I.

Right now He is seated
At the right hand of almighty God above,
But one day He'll leave the throne again
With all His glory, power, and love.

Oh, what a beautiful, glorious day
When the sky will open wide,
When we hear the trumpet of Gabriel sound,
And, on a cloud, our Jesus will ride.

He'll say, "Come, My children,
Come with Me." And away we will go.
I had to tell you so you can be ready;
I had to tell you so you'll know.

May 18, 2004

I Did It Just for You

When I'm outside and look around me
At the beautiful trees and sky so blue,
I can just hear Jesus saying,
"I did it just for you."

When I see the beauty of an autumn day
And the sunset with it's beautiful hue,
My Jesus smiles down from His home above
And says, "I did it just for you."

Can't you hear the soft sweet whisper
Deep within your heart? It's true;
As you take a look around you
As He says, "I did it just for you."

Oh, the beauty of creation!
What a wonderful Savior so true!
Open your eyes, world! Behold the beauty;
Jesus did it just for you.

We don't ever know when will be the last time
Its beauty we will see.
Know in your heart that God created it,
And He did it for you and me.

October 21, 2004

Just Traveling Through

I'm not on this earth to stay;
I'm just traveling through.
I'm looking and waiting for a better home.
How about you?

I know my Lord is preparing
A home far up above,
A home where I'll be so happy,
A home He built with His love.

He's promised me a mansion
Up in that Heavenly place
But the most important thing to me,
Is to see Him face to face.

Although I'm just traveling through
This world on which I trod,
I want to tell as many as I can
About the wonderful Home of God.

I want to carry as many with me,
As many as I can,
To a home so beautiful and serene,
For that is God's wonderful plan.

November 15, 2004

This Man Called Jesus

Some two thousand years ago,
A baby came to earth.
It was a blessed event,
The miracle of His birth.

He was born to a virgin;
Mary was her name.
The angel came to visit her,
And she was never, ever the same.

Our God in Heaven was His Father.
Although Joseph was the earthly one.
This man, Whose name is Jesus,
Is God's holy, beloved Son.

This baby was born in a stable
Because there was no room in the inn.
He came to the earth for a reason:
To save us all from our sins.

This was done according
To the plan of God above.
It was His wonderful way
Of showing us His love.

He came to give us hope
In a home so bright and fair.
Oh, I can hardly wait
To meet my Lord up there!

What a wonderful man is Jesus,
Who suffered and died that day
And then arose again
To show us all the *way*.

The *way* that we can all
Be gathered in Heaven one day,
To live forevermore
And there forever to stay.

December 14, 2004

The King of the Whole Earth

NKJV, Zechariah 14:9 — And the LORD *shall be King over all the earth. In that day it shall be — "The* LORD *is one," And His name one.*

There is coming a day
When our Lord will reign
Over the whole earth.
Every tongue will proclaim.

Every knee will bow
To the King of *all* kings.
Every voice will be raised,
His praises to sing.

There will only be one name:
Jesus! Yes, that's the one.
For He is the great I AM.
He is God's holy Son.

There are those living now
Who do not know Him,
But there will come a day
When there will be no more sin.

There will be *one* Lord,
The King of Heaven and earth.
The only Name will be Jesus,
Who gave us a new birth.

December 29, 2004
11:35 a.m.

God's Saving my Family, One by One

My precious Lord and Savior,
Oh, how faithful, my Lord is He.
He is fulfilling His promise,
One that He made to me.

He promised me in His Word,
I've read it o'er and o'er,
That He would save my children.
Oh, what a blessing I have in store!

I've seen what God is doing.
He's saving them, one by one.
They're coming and accepting
Jesus Christ, God's holy Son.

Sometimes I've gotten impatient
And thought, "Oh, God, please tell me when."
But I know He keeps His promises.
If I'm patient, He'll answer, and then

One day we'll all be together
In Heaven, my family and me.
If you will accept my Savior, too,
You'll see. Oh, yes, you will see!

February 13, 2005

My Purpose

God shaped me for a purpose,
And He expects of me
To use what He has given me
To be the best that I can be.

I must first discover
What my purpose could be,
And then, when I have found it,
To work at it diligently.

He doesn't want me to worry
About the abilities He gave others.
I'm not to ever covet those
Of my sisters and my brothers.

God has a divine purpose
For each of us, you see.
We need to pray and ask Him
What our divine purpose could be.

He will reveal it to us
If we will only stay faithful to Him.
If we continue in His Word and pray,
He will give us the answer within.

Sometimes He puts us through a trial
To reshape our lives for Him.
When we find out what our purpose is,
We'll be different than we've ever been.

The only real peace and happiness
Comes from the Father above
When we live out our purpose for Him
In the center of His love.

February 16, 2005

Thy Word, O Lord

NKJV, Psalm 19:10—More to be desired are they than gold, Yea, than much fine gold; Sweeter also than honey and the honeycomb.

NKJV, Psalm 119:105—Your Word is a lamp to my feet and a light to my path.

Thy Word, O Lord,
Is a lamp to my feet,
And Thy Word, O Lord,
Oh, it is so sweet.

Thy Word tells me
It is more precious than gold,
And Your sweet message
Will never grow old.

It is sweeter by far
Than honey from the comb,
And it lights up my path,
No matter where I roam.

I love to open Thy Word
And to seek Thy face.
It tells of Thy love
In each and every place.

If only I could tell all
How It ministers to me,

How It turned me around,
And how It set me free.

Everyone could feel
Thy sweet peace deep inside
If they would let the Holy Spirit
Come in their heart to abide.

If they would only ask Him
To lead them each day,
Their life would be much sweeter
If they would only pray.

I pray for others.
Each day as I bow,
I ask the dear Lord
To please show them how,

How they, too, can live someday
With Him throughout eternity.
Please bring them in, O Lord,
And set them free.

February 22, 2005

The Sparrow

Today as I was looking out the window,
A small sparrow flew to the ground.
As I just sat there watching,
He started hopping all around.

Do you know what God's Word says
About the sparrows that fly each day?
God tells us that we are worth more,
Much, much more, than they.

He tells us that even the hairs of our head
Are all numbered, one by one.
My! How very precious we are
To Jesus, God's holy Son.

If He loves us this much,
The greatest love known throughout the land,
And if we are worth more than a sparrow,
What a great love He has for man.

June 8, 2005

Printed in the United States
38315LVS00006B/1-135